Put wings on your phonics!

Phonics

Alphabet

Wing Wing **Phonics 1**

Published by Nexus Co., Ltd.
24, Yanghwa-ro 8-gil, Mapo-gu, Seoul 04044, Korea
www.nexusEDU.kr

Author: Nexus Contents Development Team
Publisher: Yongbaeg Ahn
ISBN: 978-89-93164-03-9 68740
      978-89-93164-06-0 (set)
Copyright © 2008 by Nexus Co., Ltd.

Printed in Korea ⑨

Put wings on your phonics!

Wing Wing Phonics 1

Alphabet

Nexus Contents Development Team

NEXUS Edu

Contents

Unit 1 Aa, Bb, Cc

 Look & Say

 Listen and point to the words. track 01

Listen & Say

 Listen and repeat.

A a

apple

ant

arm

B b

boy

book

bag

C c

cat

cap

cup

Listen and circle.

Aa Cc   Bb Cc   Bb Aa

Write & Say

 Read, trace and write.

A A A

a a

B B B

b b b

C C C

c c c

 Trace and write.

Aa Aa

Bb Bb

Cc Cc

 **Listen & Do**

 Listen and circle.

bag	apple	cat
boy	arm	cap
ant	book	cup

 Listen and circle.

A	b	c	a	B	C
a	b	C	A	B	c

Read & Do

 Read, find and say.

A is for ... .

B is for ... .

C is for ... .

Look & Do

ABC Look and place the stickers.

Unit 2 Dd, Ee, Ff

 ## Look & Say

 Listen and point to the words.   track 02

Listen & Say

 Listen and repeat.

Dd

dog

door

doll

Ee

elephant

egg

elbow

Ff

fish

frog

fox

 Listen and circle.

Ee Ff   Dd Ee   Ff Dd

13

Write & Say

 Read, trace and write.

D D

d d

E E

e e

F F

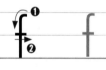

f f

 Trace and write.

Dd Dd

Ee Ee

Ff Ff

14

Listen & Do

Listen and circle.

dog

egg

fox

frog

door

elephant

elbow

fish

doll

 Listen and circle.

D   e   f   d   E   F

d   e   F   d   E   f

Read & Do

 Read, find and say.

D is for .

E is for .

F is for

16

Look & Do

ABC Look and place the stickers.

Review

1 Listen and circle. track 03

A b F c D e F C a

2 Listen, circle and write the first letters.

_____
_____
_____

_____
_____
_____

_____
_____
_____

_____
_____
_____

_____
_____
_____

_____
_____
_____

3 Match.

B D F A E C

f a b c d e

4 Look and match.

C e

E b

B c

5 Look and circle.

a B f   C d F   e A c

6 Circle the correct picture.

A a

D d

F f

Look, circle and write.

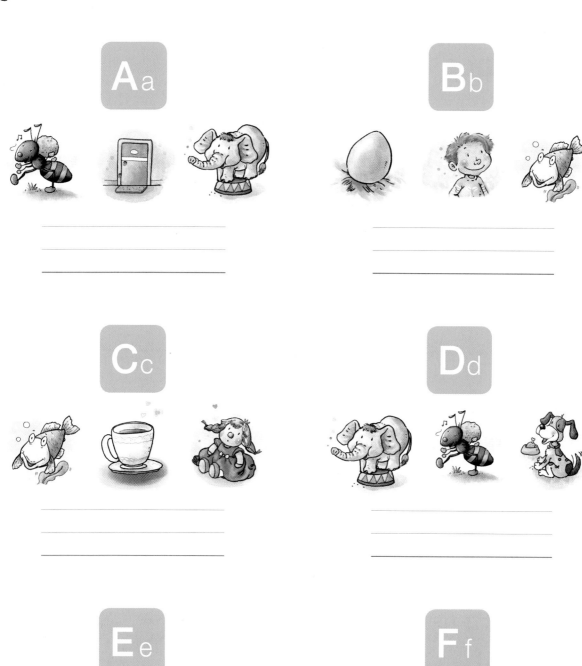

Unit 3 Gg, Hh, Ii

Look & Say

 Listen and point to the words.   track 04

22

Listen & Say

 Listen and repeat. 🎧

 Gg

girl   goat   goose

 Hh

hat   ham   hen

 **Ii**

ink   insect   igloo

 Listen and circle. 🎧

Hh   Gg   Gg   Ii   Ii   Hh

Write & Say

 Read, trace and write.

G G

g g

H H

h h

I I

i i

 Trace and write.

Gg Gg

Hh Hh

Ii Ii

 **Listen & Do**

 Listen and circle.

igloo

goat

hen

goose

hat

insect

girl

ham

ink

 Listen and circle.

G   h   i   g   H   i

g   H   I   G   h   I

25

Read & Do

 Read, find and say.

G is for   .

H is for

I is for   .

Look & Do

ABC   Look and place the stickers.

Unit 4 Jj, Kk, Ll

 ## Look & Say

 Listen and point to the words.   track 05

Listen & Say

 Listen and repeat.

J j

jam   jacket   jump

K k

king   key   kitten

L l

lamp   lion   lemon

 Listen and circle.

J j   L l   K k   L l   K k   J j

Write & Say

 Read, trace and write.

 Trace and write.

Listen & Do

 Listen and circle. 🎧

lemon   kitten   jump

jacket   lion   key

king   jam   lamp

 Listen and circle. 🎧

J   k   L   l   K   j

K   j   L   L   k   j

 # Read & Do

 Read, find and say.

J is for   .

K is for   .

L is for

 # Look & Do

ABC Look and place the stickers.

1 Listen and circle. track 06

H I I J k i G I h k

2 Listen, circle and write the first letters.

_____   _____

_____   _____

_____   _____

_____   _____

_____   _____

_____   _____

3 Match.

H　　L　　J　　G　　I　　K

j　　i　　h　　k　　l　　g

4 Look and match.

5 Look and circle.

i J H   g j K   h L j

6 Circle the correct picture.

7 Look, circle and write.

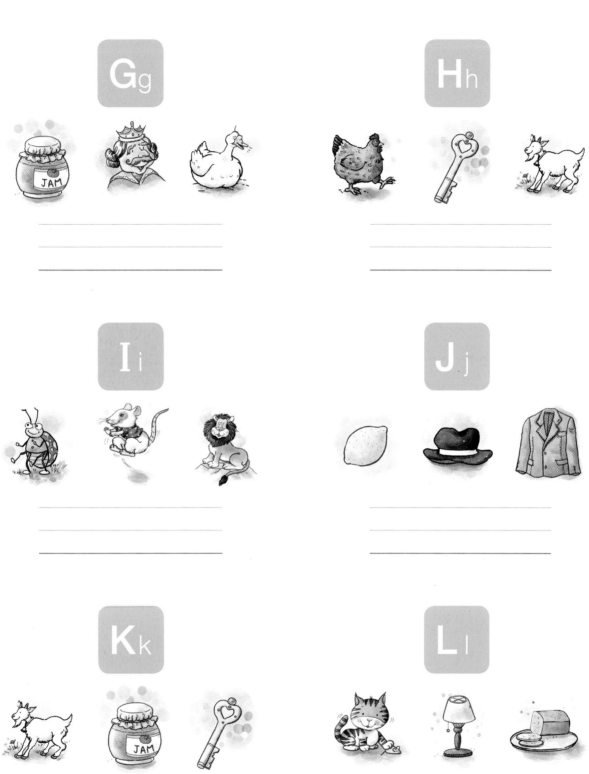

G g

_____

H h

_____

I i

_____

J j

_____

K k

_____

L l

_____

Unit 5 Mm, Nn, Oo

 Look & Say

 Listen and point to the words. track 07

Listen & Say

 Listen and repeat.

 **Mm**

mouse   moon   monkey

Nn

net   nest   nut

Oo

octopus   owl   ox

 Listen and circle.

Mm Oo   Nn Oo   Nn Mm

Write & Say

 Read, trace and write.

M M

m m

N N

n n

O O

o o

 Trace and write.

Mm Mm

Nn Nn

Oo Oo

 **Listen & Do**

 Listen and circle.

moon

nut

owl

nest

ox

mouse

octopus

monkey

net

 Listen and circle.

M   o   n   N   m   O

o   n   M   n   o   M

Read & Do

Read, find and say.

M is for   .

N is for .

O is for .

Look & Do

ABC Look and place the stickers.

Look & Say

 Listen and point to the words. track 08

Listen & Say

 Listen and repeat.

Pp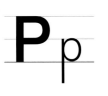

pig   pan   pot

Qq

queen   quilt   question

Rr

rose   ring   rabbit

 Listen and circle.

Qq   Pp   Rr   Qq   Pp   Rr

Write & Say

 Read, trace and write.

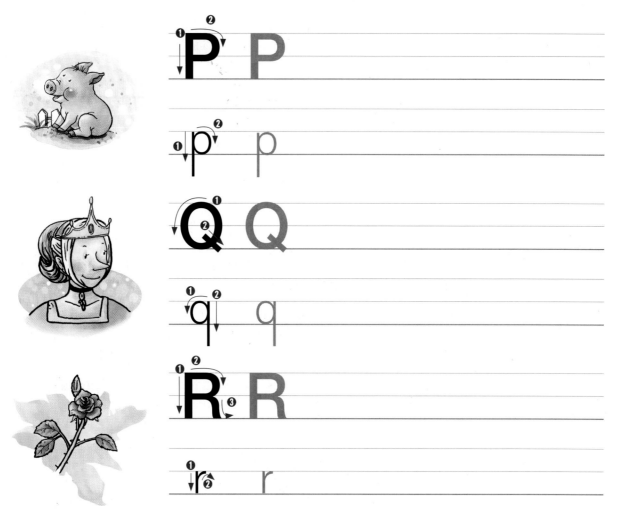

 Trace and write.

Pp Pp

Qq Qq

Rr Rr

 # Listen & Do

 Listen and circle.

pig

ring

queen

question

pot

rabbit

rose

quilt

pan

 Listen and circle.

P   q   r   R   Q   p

q   p   R   Q   r   P

Read & Do

 Read, find and say.

P is for   .   R is for   .

Q is for

 # Look & Do

ABC Look and place the stickers.

1 Listen and circle. track 09

M N o p q R n r O

2 Listen, circle and write the first letters. 🎧

_____

_____

_____

_____

_____

_____

_____

_____

_____

_____

_____

_____

_____

_____

_____

_____

_____

_____

Match.

4 Look and match.

5 Look and circle.

o **N** R   n **Q** m   r **N** p

6 Circle the correct picture.

O o

M m

R r

Look, circle and write.

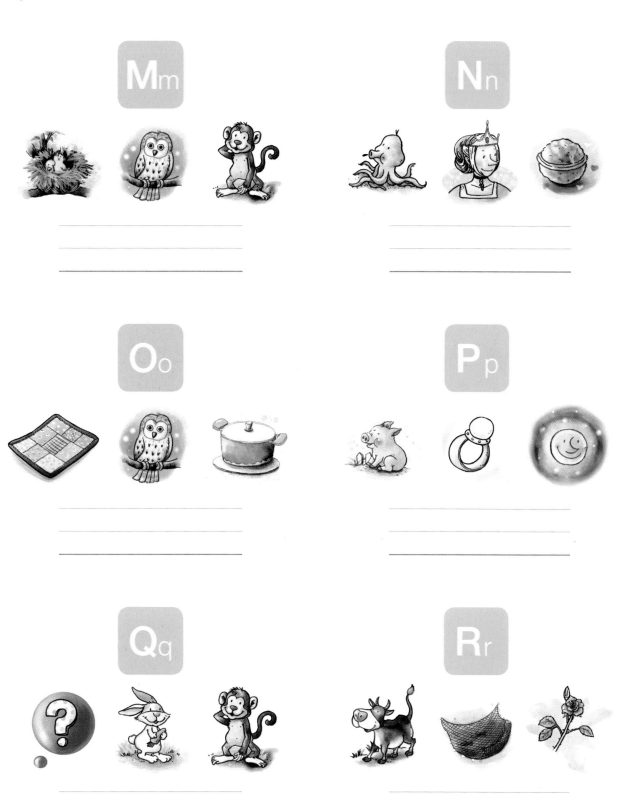

Unit 7 Ss, Tt, Uu, Vv

 Look & Say

 Listen and point to the words. track 10

Listen & Say

Listen and repeat.

S s

sun

sea

ship

T t

tree

toy

table

U u

umbrella

uncle

under

V v

vest

vase

violin

Write & Say

 Read, trace and write.

Listen & Do

 Listen and circle.

toy   uncle   vase

vest   table   sun

umbrella   violin   tree

Listen and circle.

S   t   V   T   v   s

u   T   s   U   t   V

57

Read & Do

 Read, find and say.

S is for   . 　　T is for   .

Look & Do

Look and place the stickers.

Unit 8 Ww, Xx, Yy, Zz

 ## Look & Say

 Listen and point to the words.   track 11

Listen & Say

 Listen and repeat.

W w

window   water   watch

X x

box   six   ax

Y y

yellow   yo-yo   yacht

Z z

zoo   zero   zebra

Write & Say

 Read, trace and write.

 **Listen & Do**

 Listen and circle.

window

yo-yo

zebra

yacht

water

box

zoo

yellow

six

 Listen and circle.

W y x   z w X

y z W   x Y Z

Read & Do

 Read, find and say.

W is for   . X is for   .

Y is for   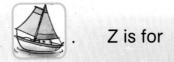 . Z is for   .

 # Look & Do

ABC Look and place the stickers.

Review

1 Listen and circle. track 12

| S | y | X | | V | w | U |
| t | Z | v | | W | x | Y |

2 Listen and circle.

| zero | yo-yo | box | ax |

| tree | umbrella | violin | sea |

| ship | six | window | uncle |

| vase | yacht | zoo | table |

3 Match.

(T) (Y) (X) (V) (S) (W) (Z) (U)

(v) (w) (z) (t) (y) (u) (x) (s)

4 Look and match.

V

Z

Z

X

X

V

5 Look and circle.

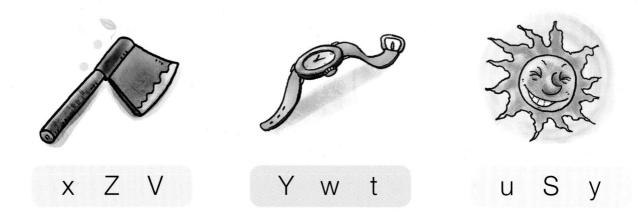

x Z V   Y w t   u S y

6 Circle the correct picture.

W w

U u

S s

7 Look and write the first letters.

_____

_____

_____

_____

_____

_____

_____

_____

Alphabet Song

 Sing and place the stickers.

memo~

B b   A a

D d   C c

F f   E e

H h   G g

J j

I i

L l

K k

N n

M m

P p   O o

R r   Q q

T t   S s

Yellow

ZOO

V v

U u

X x

W w

Z z

Y y

Aa Aa Aa   Dd Dd Dd   Gg Gg Gg

Bb Bb Bb   Ee Ee Ee   Hh Hh Hh

Cc Cc Cc   Ff Ff Ff   Ii Ii Ii

Jj Jj Jj   Mm Mm Mm   Pp Pp Pp

Kk Kk Kk   Nn Nn Nn   Qq Qq Qq

Ll Ll Ll   Oo Oo Oo   Rr Rr Rr

Ss Ss Ss   Ww Ww Ww

Tt Tt Tt   Xx Xx Xx

Uu Uu Uu   Yy Yy Yy

Vv Vv Vv   Zz Zz Zz

Aa Bb Cc Dd Ee Ff Gg Hh Ii

Jj Kk Ll Mm Nn Oo Pp Qq Rr

Ss Tt Uu Vv Ww Xx Yy Zz

Put wings on your phonics!

Wing Wing

1

Phonics

Workbook

Alphabet

Nexus Contents Development Team

NEXUS Edu

Put wings on your phonics!

Wing Wing

Phonics

1

Alphabet

Nexus Contents Development Team

Workbook

NEXUS Edu

Unit **1** Aa, Bb, Cc

Trace and write.

apple

ant

arm

Aa **A**a

boy

book

bag

Bb **B**b

cat

cup

cap

Cc **C**c

Look and circle.

 Look and match.

B   **A**   **C**

a   **c**   **b**

Write the partner letter.

A _____ **b** **C**

B **A** c

a **C** b

Ladder Game

Unit 2 Dd, Ee, Ff

 Trace and write.

D d

dog   door   doll

Dd Dd

E e

elephant   egg   elbow

Ee Ee

F f

fish   frog   fox

Ff Ff

Look and circle.

 Look and match.

E   F   D

f   d   e

Write the partner letter.

F

d

E

D

E

f

f

D

e

Match and write.

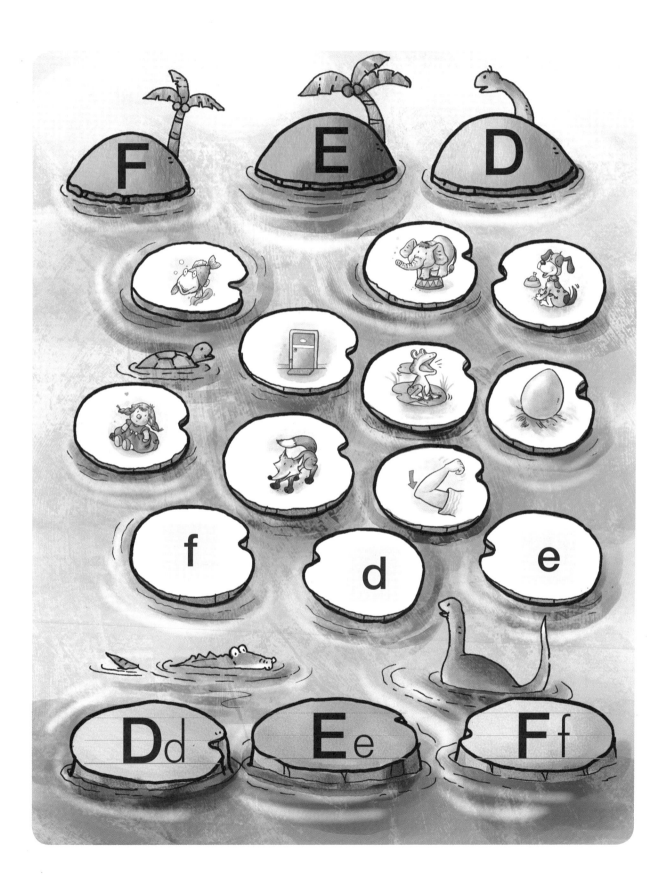

Trace and write.

Gg

girl

goat

goose

Gg Gg

Hh

hat

ham

hen

Hh Hh

Ii

ink

insect

igloo

Ii Ii

Look and circle.

I i	**H** h	**G** g

 Look and match.

•　　　　　•　　　　　•

•　　　　　•　　　　　•

I　　　　**H**　　　　**G**

•　　　　　•　　　　　•

g　　　　h　　　　i

Write the partner letter.

G   **I**   h

H   g   i

I   **H**   g

Ladder Game

Unit 4 Jj, Kk, Ll

Trace and write.

J j

jam

jacket

jump

Jj **J**j

K k

king

key

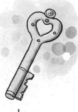
kitten

Kk **K**k

L l

lamp

lion

lemon

Ll **L**l

Look and circle.

K k	J j	L l

 Look and match.

L   K   J

j   l   k

Write the partner letter.

 **K**

 **J**

 **l**

 **j**

 **K**

 **L**

 **l**

 **k**

 **J**

Match and write.

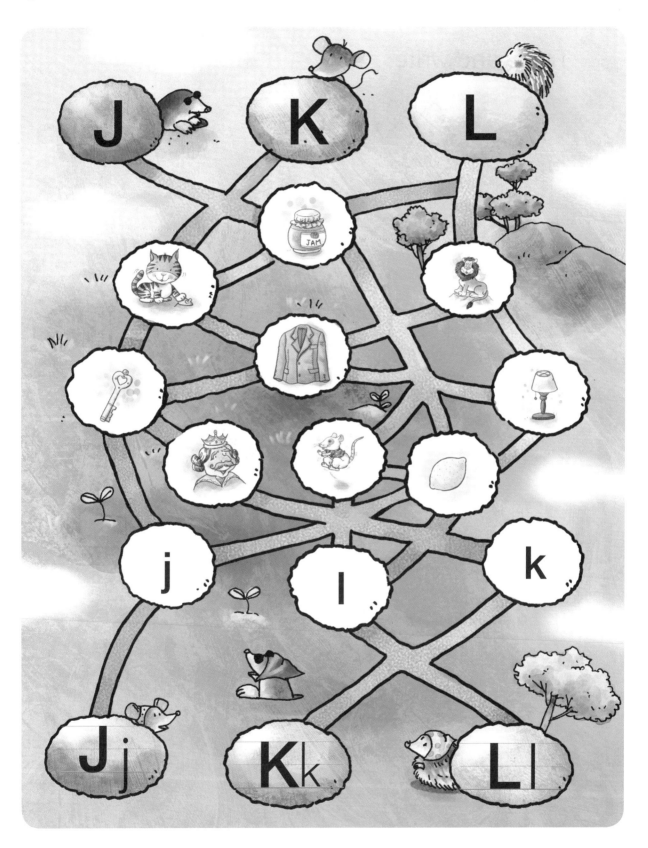

Unit 5 Mm, Nn, Oo

 Trace and write.

Mm

mouse   moon   monkey

Mm Mm

Nn

net   nest   nut

Nn Nn

Oo

octopus   owl   ox

Oo Oo

Look and circle.

 Look and match.

M   N   O

o   m   n

Write the partner letter.

M   N   o

n   O   M

o   m   N

Follow the way.

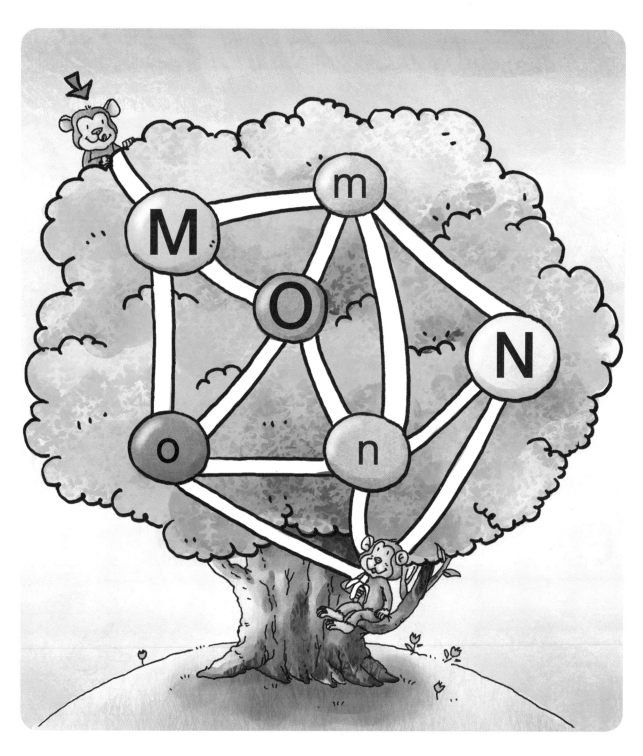

Unit 6 Pp, Qq, Rr

✏️ Trace and write.

pig

pan

pot

Pp **P**p

queen

quilt

question

Qq **Q**q

rose

ring

rabbit

Rr **R**r

Look and circle.

Q q

P p

R r

 Look and match.

P

R

Q

q

p

r

Write the partner letter.

Q _____

_____ r _____

r **P** _____

_____ p _____

_____ q _____

_____ **R** _____

_____ r _____

_____ **P** _____

_____ **Q** _____

Match and write.

Unit 7 Ss, Tt, Uu, Vv

✏️ **Trace and write.**

sun

sea

ship

S s S s

tree

toy

table

T t T t

umbrella

uncle

under

U u U u

vest

vase

violin

V v V v

Look and circle.

 Look and match.

U

T

S

t

u

s

Write the partner letter.

T   u   V

v   S   T

s   U   v

Choose and write the numbers.

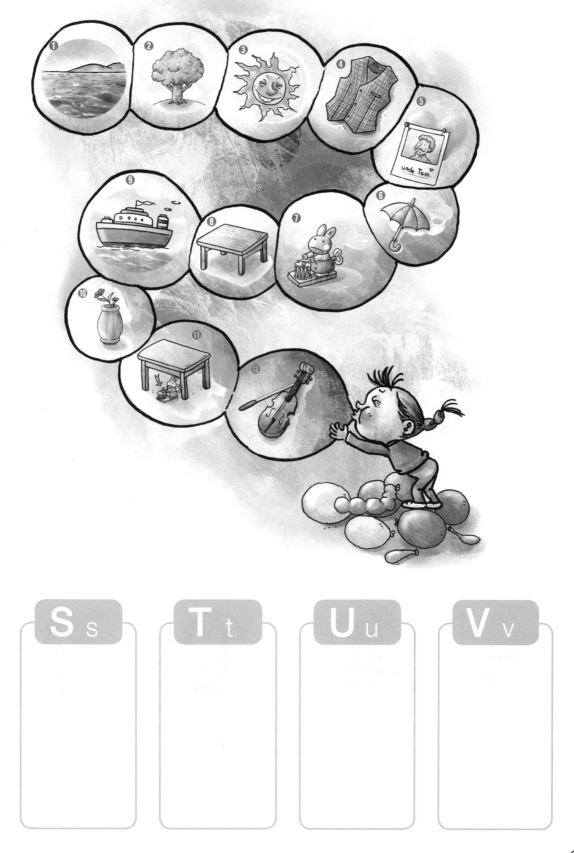

S s	T t	U u	V v

Unit 8 Ww, Xx, Yy, Zz

Trace and write.

 **Ww**

window

water

watch

WwWw

 **Xx**

box

six

ax

XxXx

 **Yy**

yellow

yo-yo

yacht

YyYy

 **Zz**

zoo

zero

zebra

ZzZz

Look and circle.

Y y	W w	Z z

 Look and match.

X Y W

y w x

Write the partner letter.

Y _____ _____ W **X** _____

_____ x **Z** _____ _____ y

_____ z **W** _____ **X** _____

Choose and write the numbers.

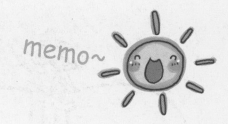

memo~

Wing Wing Phonics ①

Wing Wing Phonics is a three-book phonics series designed for elementary school students. The main purpose of this phonics series is to develop basic English sounds through a systematic presentation of the alphabet, vowel combinations, and consonant blends. The series has charming, full-color illustrations and a variety of activities that will stimulate the learners' interest.

 ## Features

· Activities to build listening skills
· Review units featuring fun games
· Chants and stories to review sounds, letters, and words
· A test included in the Teacher's Materials
· A colorful illustrated glossary of key vocabularies
· An accompanying individual workbook with writing activities

 ## Components of the Series

· Wing Wing Phonics 1 Alphabet
· Wing Wing Phonics 2 Single Letter Sounds
· Wing Wing Phonics 3 Long Vowels & Double Letter Sounds

1

Put wings on your phonics!

Wing Wing

Phonics

Answers

Alphabet

Put wings on your phonics!

Wing Wing

Phonics

Alphabet

1

Answers

NEXUS Edu

Unit 1 — Aa, Bb, Cc

Look & Say
Listen and point to the words.

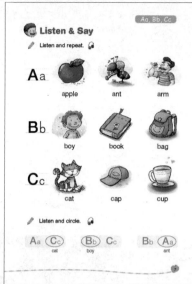

Listen & Say
Listen and repeat.

Aa — apple, ant, arm

Bb — boy, book, bag

Cc — cat, cap, cup

Listen and circle.

Aa (Cc) — cat   (Bb) Cc — boy   Bb (Aa) — ant

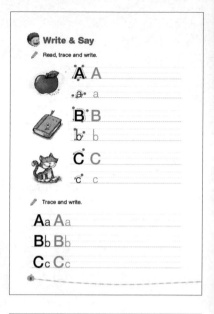

Write & Say
Read, trace and write.

A A — apple
a a

B B — book
b b

C C — cat
c c

Trace and write.

Aa Aa
Bb Bb
Cc Cc

Listen & Do
Listen and circle.

bag — apple — cat

boy — arm — cap

ant — book — cup

Listen and circle.

A b (c) cap   a (B) C bag
(a) b c apple   A B (c) cat

Read & Do
Read, find and say.

A is for ... Apple, Ant, Arm/A
B is for ... Boy, Book, Bag/B
C is for ... Cat, Cap, Cup/C

Look & Do
Look and place the stickers.

Unit 2 — Dd, Ee, Ff

Look & Say
Listen and point to the words.

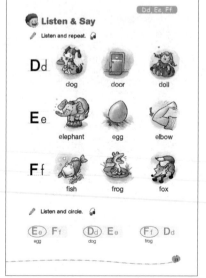

Listen & Say
Listen and repeat.

Dd — dog, door, doll

Ee — elephant, egg, elbow

Ff — fish, frog, fox

Listen and circle.

(Ee) Ff — egg   (Dd) Ee — dog   (Ff) Dd — frog

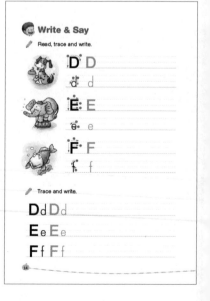

Write & Say
Read, trace and write.

D D — dog
d d

E E — elephant
e e

F F — fish
f f

Trace and write.

Dd Dd
Ee Ee
Ff Ff

2

Listen & Do

Listen and circle.

dog	egg	fox
frog	door	elephant
elbow	fish	doll

Listen and circle.

D (e) f   d E (F)
egg   fox

(d) e F   d (E) f
door   elephant

Read & Do

Read, find and say.

Look & Do

Look and place the stickers.

Review

1 Listen and circle.

A (b) F c D (e) (F) C a
book   elbow fish

2 Listen, circle and write the first letters.

Cc   Bb

Dd   Ff

Ee   Aa

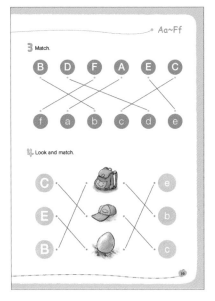

Aa~Ff

3 Match.

B D F A E C

f a b c d e

4 Look and match.

C E B

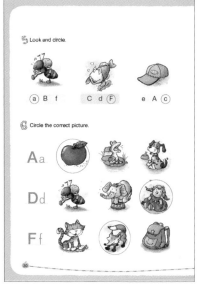

5 Look and circle.

(a) B f   C d (F)   e A (c)

6 Circle the correct picture.

Aa

Dd

Ff

7 Look, circle and write.

Aa   Bb

A a   B b

Cc   Dd

C c   D d

Ee   Ff

E e   F f

Unit 3 Gg, Hh, Ii

Look & Say

Listen and point to the words.

Gg, Hh, Ii

Listen & Say

Listen and repeat.

Gg   girl   goat   goose

Hh   hat   ham   hen

Ii   ink   insect   igloo

Listen and circle.

Hh (Gg)   Gg (Ii)   Ii (Hh)
goat   ink   hat

Write & Say

Read, trace and write.

G G G
g g
H H H
h h
I I I
i i

Trace and write.

Gg Gg
Hh Hh
Ii Ii

Listen & Do

Listen and circle.

igloo   goat   hen

goose   hat   insect

girl   ham   ink

Listen and circle.

G h (i)   g (H) i
insect   ham
(g) H I   G h (I)
goat   igloo

Read & Do

Read, find and say.

G is for

H is for

I is for

Look & Do

Look and place the stickers.

Unit 4 Jj, Kk, Ll

Look & Say

Listen and point to the words.

Jj, Kk, Ll

Listen & Say

Listen and repeat.

J j   jam   jacket   jump

K k   king   key   kitten

L l   lamp   lion   lemon

Listen and circle.

(Jj) Ll   Kk (Ll)   (Kk) Jj
jam   lion   king

Write & Say

Read, trace and write.

J J J
j j
K K K
k k
L L L
l l

Trace and write.

Jj Jj
Kk Kk
Ll Ll

Listen & Do

Listen and circle.

lemon   kitten   jump

jacket   lion   key

king   jam   lamp

Listen and circle.

(J) k L   l (K) j
jam   key
K j (L)   L k (j)
     lamp   jump

Read & Do

Read, find and say.

J is for

K is for

L is for

Look & Do

ABC Look and place the stickers.

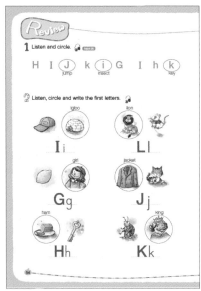

Review

1 Listen and circle. Track 33

H I **J** k **i** G I h **k**
jump   insect   key

2 Listen, circle and write the first letters.

igloo / cap   lion / mouse

I i   **L** l

lemon / girl   jacket / cat

G g   **J** j

ham / hat   king / insect

H h   **K** k

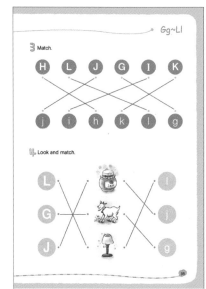

Gg~Ll

3 Match.

H L J G I K

j i h k l g

4 Look and match.

L   l
G   j
J   g

5 Look and circle.

i J H   g j **K**   h L **j**

6 Circle the correct picture.

I i

L l

G g

7 Look, circle and write.

G g

H h

I i

J j

K k

L l

Unit 5 Mm, Nn, Oo

Look & Say

Listen and point to the words. Track 37

M, moon

Mm, Nn, Oo

Listen & Say

Listen and repeat.

M m   mouse   moon   monkey

N n   net   nest   nut

O o   octopus   owl   ox

Listen and circle.

M m   O o   N n   **O** o   **N** n   M m
moon   octopus   net

Write & Say

Read, trace and write.

M M

m m

N N

n n

O O

o o

Trace and write.

M m M m

N n N n

O o O o

Listen & Do

Listen and circle.

moon   nut   owl

nest   ox   mouse

octopus   monkey   net

Listen and circle.

M **o** n   **N** m O
owl   nest

o n **M**   n o M
moon   ox

5

Read & Do

Read, find and say.

M is for

N is for

O is for

Look & Do

Look and place the stickers.

Look & Say

Listen and point to the words.

Listen & Say

Pp, Qq, Rr

Listen and repeat.

Pp pig pan pot

Qq queen quilt question

Rr rose ring rabbit

Listen and circle.

Qq (Pp) pig   Rr (Qq) queen   Pp (Rr) ring

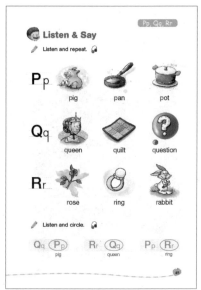

Write & Say

Read, trace and write.

P P

p p

Q Q

q q

R R

r r

Trace and write.

Pp Pp

Qq Qq

Rr Rr

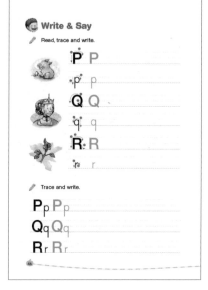

Listen & Do

Listen and circle.

pig   ring   queen

question   pot   rabbit

rose   quilt   pan

Listen and circle.

(P) q r pan   R (Q) p quilt

q p (R) rabbit   Q r (P) pot

Read & Do

Read, find and say.

P is for   R is for

Q is for

Look & Do

Look and place the stickers.

Review

1 Listen and circle.

M (N) o p q R n r (O)
    net   pig   ox

2 Listen, circle and write the first letters.

nest   pot
Nn   **Pp**
        queen

octopus
Oo   **Qq**

monkey rabbit
Mm   **Rr**

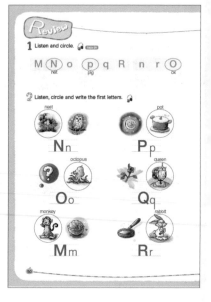

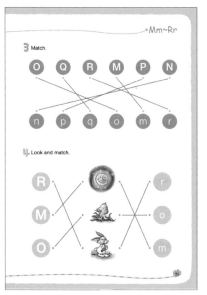

3 Match.

O Q R M P N

n p q o m r

4 Look and match.

R r

M o

O m

5 Look and circle.

o N R | n Q m | r N p

6 Circle the correct picture.

O o

M m

R r

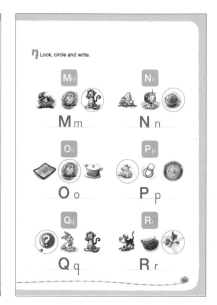

7 Look, circle and write.

M m

N n

O o

P p

Q q

R r

Unit 7 Ss, Tt, Uu, Vv

Look & Say

Listen and point to the words.

S O S

Ss, Tt, Uu, Vv

Listen & Say

Listen and repeat.

S s — sun, sea, ship

T t — tree, toy, table

U u — umbrella, uncle, under

V v — vest, vase, violin

Write & Say

Read, trace and write.

S S
s s

T T
t t

U U
u u

V V
v v

Listen & Do

Listen and circle.

toy | uncle | vase

vest | table | sun

umbrella | violin | tree

Listen and circle.

S t V | T v s
sun | violin

u T s | U t V
toy | under

Read & Do

Read, find and say.

S is for ... Sun, Sea, Ship/S

T is for ... Tree, Toy, Table/T

U is for ... Umbrella, Uncle, Under/U

V is for ... Vest, Violin, V

Look & Do

Look and place the stickers.

Ss
Ss
Ss
S O S
Tt
V
Tt
Uu
Uu
Vv
Vv
Tt

7

Unit 8 Ww, Xx, Yy, Zz

Look & Say

Listen and point to the words.

Listen & Say

Listen and repeat.

Ww	window	water	watch
Xx	box	six	ax
Yy	yellow	yo-yo	yacht
Zz	zoo	zero	zebra

Write & Say

Read, trace and write.

W W w w

X X x x

Y Y y y

Z Z z z

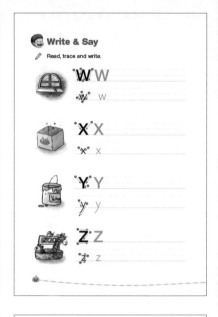

Listen & Do

Listen and circle.

window   yo-yo   zebra

yacht   water   box

zoo   yellow   six

Listen and circle.

W	y	(x) box		(z) zoo	w	X
y	z	(W) watch		x	(Y) yacht	Z

Read & Do

Read, find and say.

W is for ... Window, Water, Watch/it W

X is for ... Box, Six, Ax/it X

Y is for ... Yellow, Yo-yo, Yacht/it Y

Z is for ... Zoo, Zero, Zebra/it Z

Look & Do

Look and place the stickers.

Review

1 Listen and circle.

S	(y) yo-yo	X		V	w	(U) uncle
(t) toy	Z	v		(W) water	x	Y

2 Listen and circle.

zero   yo-yo   box   ax

tree   umbrella   violin   sea

ship   six   window   uncle

vase   yacht   zoo   table

Ss~Zz

3 Match.

T Y X V S W Z U

v w z t y u x s

4 Look and match.

V

Z

X

Z

X

V

5 Look and circle.

(x) Z V	Y (w) t	u (S) y

6 Circle the correct picture.

Ww

Uu

Ss

8

Look and write the first letters.

Y y
U u
Z z
S s
W w
V v
T t
X x

Unit 1 Aa, Bb, Cc

Trace and write.

Aa — apple — ant — arm

AaAa

Bb — boy — book — bag

BbBb

Cc — cat — cup — cap

CcCc

2

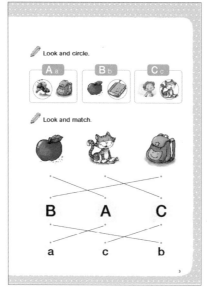

Look and circle.

Aa   Bb   Cc

Look and match.

B   A   C

a   c   b

3

Write the partner letter.

A a   B b   C c

B b   A a   C c

A a   C c   B b

4

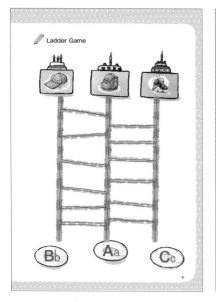

Ladder Game

Bb   Aa   Cc

5

Unit 2 Dd, Ee, Ff

Trace and write.

Dd — dog — door — doll

DdDd

Ee — elephant — egg — elbow

EeEe

Ff — fish — frog — fox

FfFf

6

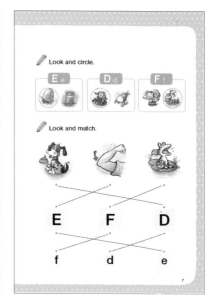

Look and circle.

Ee   Dd   Ff

Look and match.

E   F   D

f   d   e

7

🖊 Write the partner letter.

F f   D d   E e

D d   E e   F f

F f   D d   E e

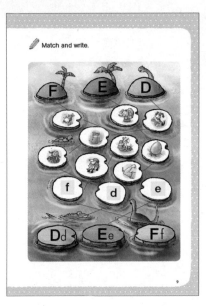

🖊 Match and write.

F E D

f d e

D d   E e   F f

Unit 3 Gg, Hh, Ii

🖊 Trace and write.

Gg   girl   goat   goose

Gg Gg

Hh   hat   ham   hen

Hh Hh

Ii   ink   insect   igloo

Ii Ii

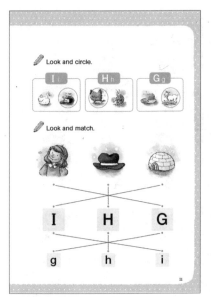

🖊 Look and circle.

I i   H h   G g

🖊 Look and match.

I   H   G

g   h   i

🖊 Write the partner letter.

G g   I i   H h

H h   G g   I i

I i   H h   G g

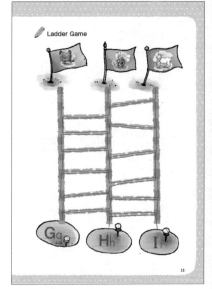

🖊 Ladder Game

Gg   Hh   Ii

Unit 4 Jj, Kk, Ll

🖊 Trace and write.

Jj   jam   jacket   jump

Jj Jj

Kk   king   key   kitten

Kk Kk

Ll   lamp   lion   lemon

Ll Ll

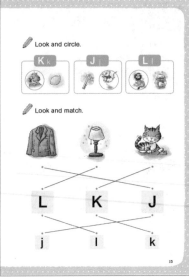

🖊 Look and circle.

K k   J j   L l

🖊 Look and match.

L   K   J

j   l   k

🖊 Write the partner letter.

K k   J j   L l

J j   K k   L l

L l   K k   J j

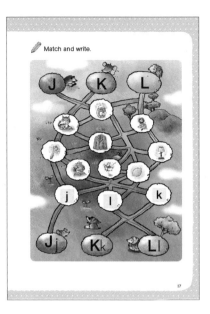

Match and write.

Unit 5 Mm, Nn, Oo

Trace and write.

Mm mouse moon monkey

MmMm

Nn net nest nut

NnNn

Oo octopus owl ox

OoOo

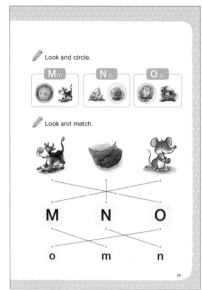

Look and circle.

Mm   Nn   Oo

Look and match.

M   N   O

o   m   n

Write the partner letter.

M m   N n   O o

N n   O o   M m

O o   M m   N n

Follow the way.

M   m

O   N

o   n

Mm   Nn   Oo

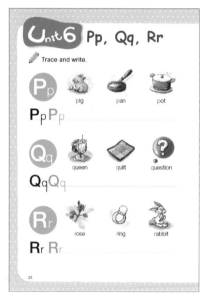

Unit 6 Pp, Qq, Rr

Trace and write.

Pp pig pan pot

PpPp

Qq queen quilt question

QqQq

Rr rose ring rabbit

RrRr

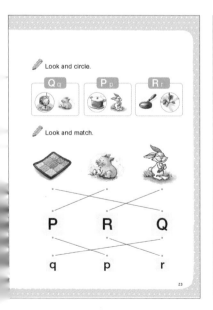

Look and circle.

Qq   Pp   Rr

Look and match.

P   R   Q

q   p   r

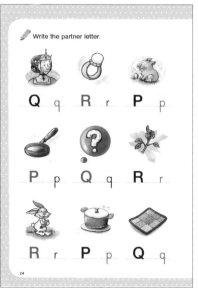

Write the partner letter.

Q q   R r   P p

P p   Q q   R r

R r   P p   Q q

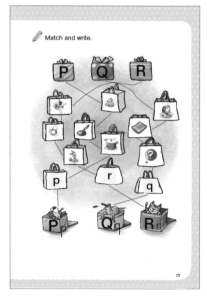

Match and write.

P   Q   R

p   r   q

P   Q   R

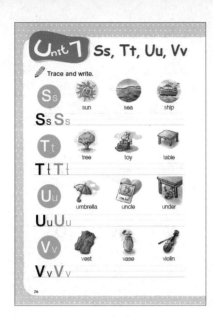

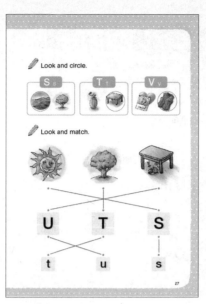

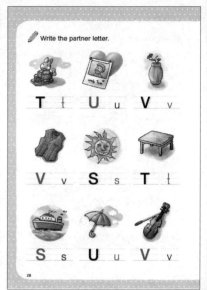

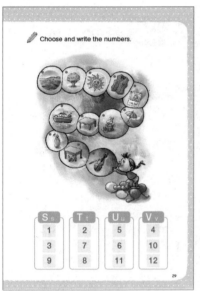

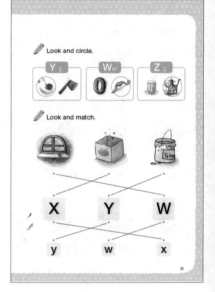